JAYSON TATUM

BY MARY BOONE

Apex is distributed by North Star Editions:
sales@northstareditions.com | 888-417-0195

Produced for Apex by Red Line Editorial.

Photographs ©: Winslow Townson/AP Images, cover, 18; Mary Schwalm/AP Images, 1, 22–23; Steven Senne/AP Images, 4–5, 6–7, 8, 26–27; Shutterstock Images, 10–11, 16–17, 19, 25; Gregory Payan/AP Images, 12; Jacob Kupferman/Cal Sport Media/AP Images, 14–15; Tony Dejak/AP Images, 21; Lynne Sladky/AP Images, 24, 29

Library of Congress Control Number: 2022923923

ISBN
978-1-63738-560-9 (hardcover)
978-1-63738-614-9 (paperback)
978-1-63738-718-4 (ebook pdf)
978-1-63738-668-2 (hosted ebook)

Printed in the United States of America
Mankato, MN
082023

NOTE TO PARENTS AND EDUCATORS

Apex books are designed to build literacy skills in striving readers. Exciting, high-interest content attracts and holds readers' attention. The text is carefully leveled to allow students to achieve success quickly. Additional features, such as bolded glossary words for difficult terms, help build comprehension.

TABLE OF CONTENTS

CHAPTER 1

CLUTCH PLAY

It's the first round of the NBA **playoffs**. The Boston Celtics are one point behind the Brooklyn Nets. The game has less than a minute left.

The Boston Celtics played the Brooklyn Nets on April 17, 2022.

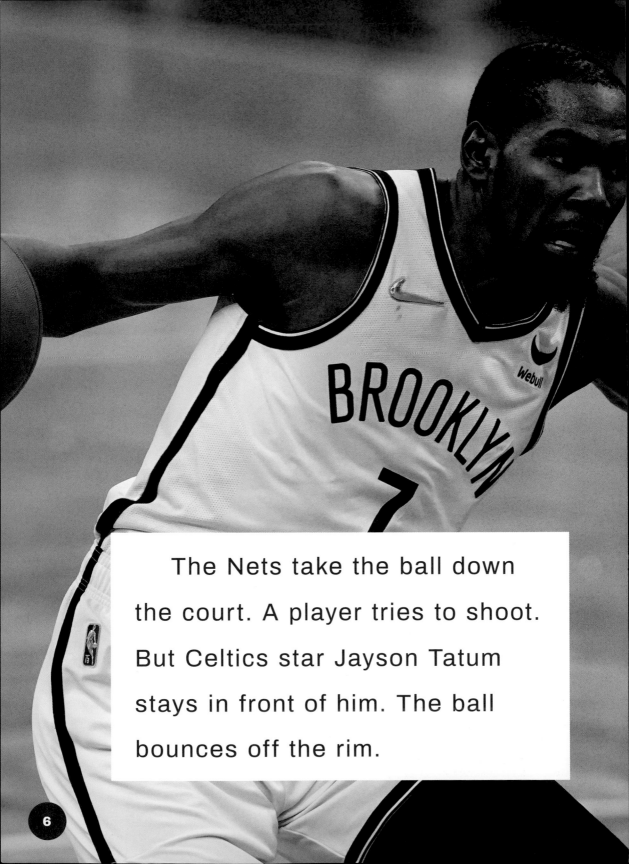

The Nets take the ball down the court. A player tries to shoot. But Celtics star Jayson Tatum stays in front of him. The ball bounces off the rim.

Jayson Tatum (right) stops Kevin Durant of the Nets from driving to the basket.

FAST FACT

Tatum scored 31 points against the Nets in Game 1 of the 2022 playoffs.

Next, the Celtics get the ball. Tatum runs toward the basket. He catches a pass and spins around a **defender**. Then he makes a **layup** as time runs out.

BUZZER-BEATER

NBA basketball games are divided into four quarters. Each quarter lasts 12 minutes. Sometimes players make shots right as the time runs out. These are called buzzer-beaters.

◀ Tatum's basket gave the Celtics a 115–114 win over the Nets.

CHAPTER 2

EARLY LIFE

Jayson Tatum grew up in St. Louis, Missouri. He began playing basketball as a young child. By middle school, he could beat much older players.

Tatum was born and raised in St. Louis, Missouri.

Jayson was a star player in high school. He scored more and more points each year. Many colleges took notice.

NOTABLE NUMBERS

Jayson averaged 13.3 points per game as a high school freshman. By his senior year, his team was the best in the state. He scored 40 points in the **championship** game.

◀ **Jayson Tatum (22) drives to the hoop in a game during his senior year of high school.**

Tatum chose to play for Duke University. He soon became one of the team leaders in scoring. He also helped Duke win a **conference** championship.

FAST FACT

Jayson's dad, Justin, played **professional** basketball in the Netherlands.

Tatum jumps past a defender to dunk the basketball.

CHAPTER 3

GOING PRO

After one year at Duke, Tatum was ready to go pro. The Boston Celtics chose him in the first round of the NBA **Draft**.

The Celtics play at TD Garden in Boston, Massachusetts.

Tatum excelled in his first year with the Celtics. He made 105 three-pointers that season. It was the most ever for a Celtics **rookie**.

Tatum made 43.4 percent of his three-point shots in the 2017–18 season.

Kobe Bryant played for the Los Angeles Lakers from 1996 to 2016. He helped them win five championships.

STAR MENTOR

In 2018, Kobe Bryant invited Tatum to a workout. The former NBA star helped Tatum do drills. It was a key moment for Tatum. Bryant had been his favorite player as a kid.

The Celtics went to the playoffs in Tatum's rookie year. They made it to the Eastern Conference Finals. But they lost in seven games.

FAST FACT

Tatum averaged 18.5 points per game in the playoffs. He scored 351 points total.

Tatum was chosen for the NBA All-Rookie First Team after the 2017–18 season.

CHAPTER 4

ALL-STAR

Tatum continued to improve. He led the Celtics to the playoffs every year from 2018 to 2021. But they never reached the NBA Finals.

Tatum makes a slam dunk during a 2020 game against the Phoenix Suns.

Tatum averaged 25 points per game during the 2022 Eastern Conference Finals.

After the 2021–22 season, the Celtics reached the Conference Finals again. This time, Tatum led them to four wins. They moved on to the NBA Finals.

GOLD MEDALIST

Tatum played in the Olympics before the 2021–22 season. He learned from many great players and coaches on Team USA. Together, they won the gold medal.

The 2020 Olympics took place in Tokyo, Japan. They were held in the summer of 2021.

The Celtics faced the Golden State Warriors in the Finals. They lost in six games. But fans looked forward to more great seasons.

Tatum takes a shot over two Golden State Warriors defenders in the 2022 NBA Finals.

FAST FACT

Tatum was named an NBA All-Star four times in a row, from 2019–20 to 2022–23.

COMPREHENSION QUESTIONS

Write your answers on a separate piece of paper.

1. Write a few sentences that explain the main ideas of Chapter 3.

2. Do you think Jayson Tatum made the right choice when he left college after one year? Why or why not?

3. Which team drafted Tatum?

    A. the Brooklyn Nets

    B. the Boston Celtics

    C. the Golden State Warriors

4. If each quarter is 12 minutes, how long is a full NBA game?

    A. 48 minutes

    B. 32 minutes

    C. 24 minutes

5. What does **excelled** mean in this book?

*Tatum **excelled** in his first year with the Celtics. He made 105 three-pointers that season.*

    A. was very good at something

    B. was a fast runner

    C. was very bad at something

6. What does **invited** mean in this book?

*In 2018, Kobe Bryant **invited** Tatum to a workout. The former NBA star helped Tatum do drills.*

    A. gave someone money

    B. asked someone to do something

    C. told someone to stay away

Answer key on page 32.

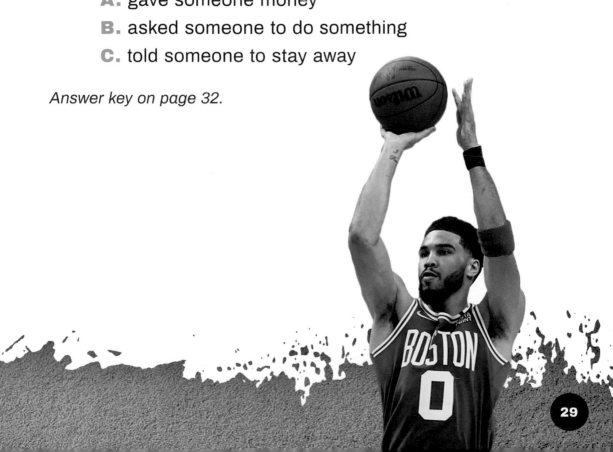

GLOSSARY

championship
The final game or series that decides the winner of a tournament.

conference
A smaller group of teams within a sports league.

defender
A player who tries to stop the other team from scoring.

draft
A system where professional teams choose new players.

layup
A one-handed shot made near the basket.

playoffs
A set of games played after the regular season to decide which team will be the champion.

professional
Having to do with people who get paid for what they do.

rookie
A player in their first year.

TO LEARN MORE

BOOKS

Flynn, Brendan. *Boston Celtics All-Time Greats*. Mendota Heights, MN: Press Box Books, 2020.

Gitlin, Marty. *Boston Celtics*. Minneapolis: Abdo Publishing, 2022.

Lilley, Matt. *The NBA Finals*. Mendota Heights, MN: Apex Editions, 2023.

ONLINE RESOURCES

Visit **www.apexeditions.com** to find links and resources related to this title.

ABOUT THE AUTHOR

Mary Boone has ridden an elephant, jumped out of an airplane, and baked dozens of cricket cookies—all in the interest of research for her books and magazine articles. She's written more than 65 nonfiction books for young readers.

INDEX

ANSWER KEY:
1. Answers will vary; 2. Answers will vary; 3. B; 4. A; 5. A; 6. B